In praise of **Hi, I'm Me in Kinder**

"A **must-have** for teachers, parents, and caregivers. *Hi, I'm Me in Kindergarten* encourages young children to use their voice to gain confidence and feel proud of their unique differences. Children will learn about acceptance, confidence, and how the power of using **kind** words and actions can positively affect others. A beautiful story of how a mother's message to her daughter helps others realize the importance of acceptance, inclusiveness, and being kind to one another."

—**Marcia Elizabeth Papa**, Early Childhood Educator,
Montessori Directress Founder/Principal,
Wee Bees Learning Centre

"It is so incredibly important to teach our children valuable lessons from an early age. This is a lovely story about going to Kindergarten and meeting new friends who at times will say something that is not so nice. Our children have a choice to accept or reject these comments. This book gives children the confidence to believe in themselves."

—**Wendy Marquenie**, Author of *Genius Asks, Who Am I?*

"Kelly Vurinaris does it again when she uses real-life lessons to teach children the importance of being kind and accepting others, even if they don't look like us. The lessons in this book are an important stepping stone toward inclusion, acceptance, and speaking up when something doesn't feel right."

—**Dr. Joanette Weisse, MD**, Author of *Giggles in my Heart* Book Series,
Founder and CEO of HartsLight Kids.

"As someone who was born with a craniofacial difference, this book resonates for me as I know it will for so many others. Kelly Vurinaris beautifully captures what it is like to be a kindergartner with a visible difference who just wants to be accepted. This book should be read by all children."

—**Dina Zuckerberg**, Director of Family Programs, myFace

Hi, I'm Me
in Kindergarten

Written by Kelly Vurinaris

Hasmark
PUBLISHING
INTERNATIONAL

Published by
Hasmark Publishing International
www.hasmarkpublishing.com

Permission should be addressed in writing to Kelly Vurinaris at haykellyv@gmail.com

Editor: Allison Burney
allison.burney@gmail.com

Design: Anne Karklins
anne@hasmarkpublishing.com

ISBN 13: 978-1-77482-053-7
ISBN 10: 1774820536

Hasmark
PUBLISHING
INTERNATIONAL

This book is dedicated to my daughter and
all the beautiful children with a unique difference.
Whatever stage of life you are in, you've got this.
Please remember to use your voice and know how important you are.

To my dear friend who has been with me on this book journey,
you've helped me discover the words that were meant to be written.
I want to thank you from the bottom of my heart.

Lastly, to my amazing husband and daughter,
we are experiencing this whole new world together, and there is
no one else I would rather be doing this with.

Hi, I'm Chloe, and I go to kindergarten.
On my first day, I was so excited to
meet new friends and learn a lot.
I was also a little scared.

I'd never had teachers before and I didn't
know anyone in my new class.
Mom said, "Remember to say, 'Hi, I'm Chloe,'"
so they'd know who I was.
I'm gonna ask them their names too.

Mom took me to the kindergarten gate
outside my new classroom and said,
"Have a fun day, sweetie. I will
pick you up when school is finished."

I gave my mom a hug and off I went with my new teacher, who took me into the classroom. I think I was very **brave** that day.

When we got to our seats, the teacher asked each of us to say our name and something special about ourselves.

I said, "My name is Chloe and I have a new puppy." Everyone was really excited that I have a new puppy!

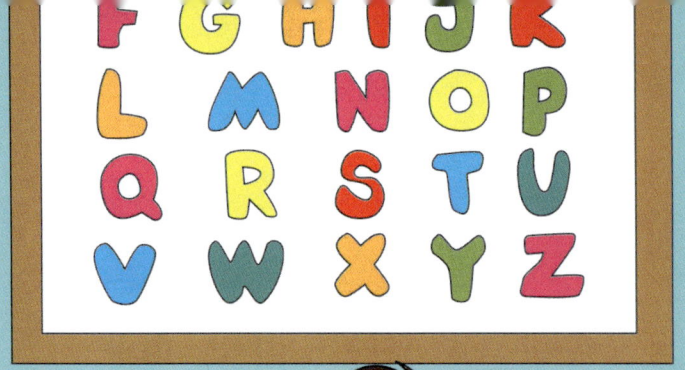

I played at the craft table
with my new friends

and found that I already knew some other kids in my class that live close to me.

Later, I got to bring home my art
to show my family. I told them about
all the fun I had.

I woke up early the next morning,
excited to get ready for school.

I even put on my favourite dress!

At the blocks centre,
a boy said,
"You look funny."
I know it's because
I look different
than he does.
It hurt my feelings.
I felt sad.

I remembered that Mom always says everyone is **different** in their own special way… and I like the way I look. I told him, "That's not nice." I also told the teacher what he said.

At dinner, I told Mom
what happened and that
it made me sad.

My mom said,
"Just because someone says
mean words doesn't mean
we have to believe them."

I always tell Mom
when I feel sad so that she
can help me feel better.

The next day in the schoolyard, I saw a girl who was sitting by herself and looked a little sad. I went to sit with her.

I shared my snack and asked if she wanted to play with me. I am so happy I did because now we play together all the time.

I really **like**
being in kindergarten

and seeing my
friends every day.

My friends like me no matter how I look, and that makes me

happy.

About the Author

Kelly Vurinaris is back with another story about acceptance and kindness, turning her debut book *Hi, I'm Me* into a series. Kelly is a mom to a beautiful daughter with Treacher-Collins Syndrome, and like in the first book, she shares the experiences her daughter and family go through in their everyday lives. As a mom, you want to protect your child in every way possible, but you can't always be there, especially when they are off to Kindergarten. Kelly believes in kindness above all and teaching kids that if you use your voice, your unknown confidence will shine through.

Join Chloe at
www.confidentlychloe.com

With every donation, a voice will be given to
the creativity that lies within the hearts of
our children living with diverse challenges.

By making this difference, children that may
not have been given the opportunity to have their
Heart Heard will have the freedom to create
beautiful works of art and musical creations.

Donate by visiting

HeartstobeHeard.com

We thank you.

Manufactured by Amazon.ca
Bolton, ON